Meeting with God

A family guide to the Christian faith

written by Nancy Gorrell
illustrated by Marianne Smith

~ From the Author ~

This book is dedicated to Crue and to Lydia, Austin and Joshua – precious sources of inspiration and joy.

With thanks to Dr Morton H. Smith, Dean of Faculty and Systematic Theology professor at Greenville Presbyterian Theological Seminary, for his careful reading and helpful suggestions.

Christian Focus Publications

Contents

Creation

Where did our world come from?
Truths about creation

Jesus

Who is Jesus?
Truths about Jesus Christ

Salvation

How can I get to heaven?
Truths about Salvation

© 2000 Nancy Gorrell
Published by Christian Focus Publications Ltd, Geanies House, Fearn, Tain, Ross-shire IV20 1TW
(www.christianfocus.com ~ email:info@christianfocus.com)

Illustrations by Marianne Smith. Written by Nancy Gorrell.

ISBN 1-85792-531-9

Scripture quotations are from The New International Version,
©1973, 1978, 1984 by the International Bible Society.

This book belongs to my family.
~ Our names are ~

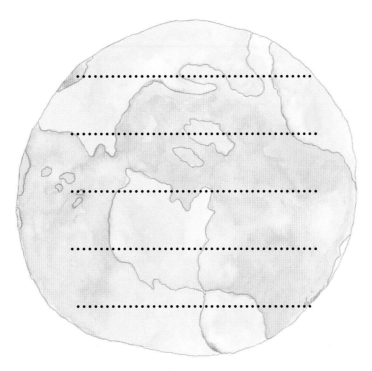

....

....

....

....

....

Look out for the memory verses at the bottom of each page.
Read and try to remember as many as you can.

Every time you learn a memory verse, you can tick a box at the end of the book.

~

As for me and my household,
we will serve the Lord.
Joshua 24:15

Creation

Can somebody tell me about Creation?

Did you ever go outside at night and see the big sky and all the stars?

Have you ever heard a bird sing? Have you touched a soft, furry rabbit? Or eaten a yummy apple?

Isn't the world wonderful and big and beautiful and exciting? "Oh, yes!" you say happily as you lie in the warm grass and watch the fluffy clouds above you.

**The heavens declare the glory of God;
the skies proclaim the work of His hands.
Psalm 19:1**

What has gone wrong with the world?

Oh no! Look out! A bee has just stung you on the nose! "Ouch! Ouch!" you say.

Sometimes the world isn't so wonderful! Sometimes you get sick or break your toys. Maybe you've even been lost or afraid of the dark.

Why do you get hurt and feel sad sometimes?

We know that the whole creation has been groaning ... right up to the present time.
Romans 8:22

Isn't the world a strange place?

One minute it's beautiful and people are happy; somewhere else, a minute later, it's dirty and ugly and people are sad.

Where did this big-beautiful-ugly-happy-sad world and the people in it come from?

In the beginning you laid the foundations of the earth.
Psalm 102:25

The world hasn't always been so messed up. God created the world as a perfect place.

The story that tells how God made the world is found in the very first book in the **Bible**, the book of **Genesis**.

God saw all that He had made, and it was very good.
Genesis 1:31

What did God make the world out of?

God's Book tells us that He made the world
out of nothing. What is nothing?

Close your eyes. You don't see anything,
do you? Well, maybe you do.

Do you see the light?
The light is something.

Do you see the dark?
The dark is something.

It's hard to think about nothing, isn't it?
But in the beginning, all that was, was
God. And God spoke words. "Let there
be light." And light was **created.**

God didn't buy a lamp and plug it in
and turn it on. He just spoke words.

By the word of the Lord were the heavens made.
Psalm 33:6

What did God do to make the world?

Isn't God amazing? Can you create something by speaking? (Try making just one little tiny ant. You couldn't do it, could you?)

But God's Bible tells us He made everything - light, darkness, sky, seas, land, plants, sun, moon, stars, birds, fish and animals - by just speaking words.

And He did it in only six days.

With my great power ... I made the earth and its people and the animals that are on it.
Jeremiah 27:5

What is the most special part of God's creation?

Do you know what the most special part of God's creation was? He formed this out of dust from the ground. Then He breathed into its nose. It was a man. When God breathed into the man, he became a living soul.

God later took a rib from the man while he was sleeping and formed a perfect friend and companion for him, a woman.

These two people would be the first parents of every other person who ever was born.

Know that the Lord is God. It is He who made us, and we are His.
Psalm 100:3

What were Adam and Eve like?

The Bible tells us that the man and woman, Adam and Eve, were made in *God's image.* They knew about God and they loved Him and obeyed Him. Adam and Eve were very happy in the place God gave them to live. It was called the Garden of Eden.

God gave the first husband and wife work to do that they enjoyed. He also gave them a very simple command to obey.

**So God created man in His own image ...
male and female He created them.
Genesis 1:27**

What did God tell Adam and Eve not to do?

He told them they must not eat from one tree that grew in their garden home, the Tree of the Knowledge of Good and Evil, or they would die.

This is a w o n d e r f u l story, isn't it? But the story doesn't end here.

Something very, very sad happened in the beautiful world that God made.

Obey me, and I will be your God and you will be my people.
Jeremiah 7:23

What did Eve do?

One day a wicked serpent, or snake, came into the pretty garden where Adam and Eve lived. (The serpent was actually **Satan,** an evil angel, in disguise.)

Satan hated God and His happy people who loved Him. He wanted to tempt them to disbelieve God's word. So he found Eve and told her lies. He told her that God really didn't mean it when He said that they would die if they disobeyed Him.

The snake also told Eve that eating the fruit from the tree would make her wiser, like God!

Oh no, Eve! Don't listen! But Eve did listen.

**Lead us not into temptation, but deliver us from the evil one.
Matthew 6:13**

What did Adam do?

Eve looked at the fruit and it looked very delicious.

She thought it might be nice to be wise about good and evil, as God was.

So Eve did what God had told her not to do. She took the fruit and ate it.

Then she gave some to Adam, and he ate it too!

Oh no, Adam! This was man's very first *sin.*

Sin entered the world through one man, and death through sin.
Romans 5:12

Think about what happens when you have done something very wrong. You feel embarrassed or guilty.

Adam and Eve were so ashamed of what they had done that they hid from God who had always been their friend.

You know my folly, O God; my guilt is not hidden from you.
Psalm 69:5

Were Adam and Eve punished?

That is how sin and sadness and death came to our world. Man brought them here.

God didn't lie when He said that Adam and Eve would be punished if they disobeyed Him.

Adam and Eve left behind a perfect and beautiful world where there was no death or sorrow, all for a piece of fruit and a greedy desire to be like God.

You may be sure that your sin will find you out.
Numbers 32:23

Am I just as bad as Adam and Eve?

Doesn't this story make you sad? It should. As Adam and Eve's great-great-great-great ... ... grandchild, you inherit their sin and misery, sadness and death.

But there's good news in this story too!

God made a promise to Adam and Eve that someone would come who would destroy Satan and sin and death. From that time on, God's people looked forward to this Special One who would come for them and save them.

**For all have sinned and fall short of the glory of God.
Romans 3:23**

Do you know who that Special One was? It was Jesus!

Jesus is the only **Saviour** from sin and death. The Saviour who was promised to the very first man and woman is the only Saviour for you today!

Christ Jesus came into the world to save sinners.
1 Timothy 1:15

Jesus did come as God had promised. You can find the story of Jesus in your Bible.

He came to give us eternal life by His obedience to God and His death on the cross. He takes those who believe in Him to a place far better than even the Garden of Eden! He takes them to heaven.

Jesus has done more for you than your first father Adam ever could have. He has given better blessings than Adam would have, even if he had obeyed God.

Isn't God amazing and kind? He can take our sorry, sad, disobedient lives, and make them beautiful and happy again. Thank God for His *grace!*

God demonstrates His own love for us in this:
While we were still sinners, Christ died for us.
Romans 5:8

Jesus

Can someone tell me about Jesus?

God's special Book, the Bible, is full of very important lessons for you. Did you know that every truth in God's Bible should help you to learn about a very wonderful person? That person is the **Lord and Saviour, Jesus Christ.**

Jesus Christ is **God's Son.** He always lived with God in heaven, even before anything you see was made!

That He is a Son does *not* mean that He was ever a little baby in heaven or even that God made Him one day before God made anything else.

What does it mean?

The Father has sent His Son to be the Saviour of the world.
1 John 4:14

What is Jesus like?

When you go to see your grandma, does she squeeze your cheeks and say, "Ooo, you look just like your daddy"? Maybe you do look like your dad. Maybe someday you will look and act like your father does now.

Jesus is *exactly* like God His Father. He is powerful like God; He has always lived, just like His Father has. All the things that make God His Father special make Jesus special too!

They are the **same**, and yet they are **two different persons**.

For the Father loves the Son and shows Him all He does.
John 5:20

What did God give Jesus for His very own?

Before God ever made the world, He gave His only Son Jesus a wonderful gift.

He gave Jesus a special group of people that He would create to be Jesus' very own.

They were yours; you gave them to me.
John 17:6

Does Jesus love me?

Jesus loves His people very much, so He wanted them to come to heaven to be with Him.

But He knew that His people did not love Him. They did wrong things and could not come to God's perfect home, heaven.

So Jesus had to do a very hard job.

**Father, I want those you have given me
to be with me where I am, and to see my glory.
John 17:24**

How did Jesus come to earth?

Jesus had to be born on earth as a baby, just as you were born!

This is called the ***incarnation***. God's Son took a body and became a real man.

Then Jesus had to live a perfect life. He never stole anything or was unhappy with the things He had, even though He was very poor while He lived on the earth. He never beat up His little brothers and sisters, or lied, or said unkind words, or even thought bad things!

**Today in the town of David a Saviour has been born to you;
He is Christ the Lord.
Luke 2:11**

How did Jesus die?

When Jesus became a grown-up man, He worked very hard to teach people about God.

Sometimes people hated Him or hurt Him or made Him sad, but He did not quit.

Then Jesus had to die a very terrible and painful death on the cross. Some people even laughed at Him and were unkind to Him while He was dying!

But during all this, Jesus never did anything to displease His Father.

They crucified him, along with the criminals.
Luke 23:33

Why did Jesus die?

But why did Jesus have to do all this? That is a very good question.

Jesus did all these things for His people whom He loves. Jesus knew that His little children could not be perfect, so He was perfect for them! Then He died for them so that God would not have to punish them for the bad things they do.

Jesus took their place. He was their *substitute*.

Christ died for our sins.
1 Corinthians 15:3

What happened after Jesus died?

God was happy with Jesus and what He had done.

After Jesus' body had been in a grave for three days, God raised Him from the dead! This is called the *resurrection*.

Jesus showed Himself to His disciples and then went back to His Father. Even though He is now high in the heavens with God, He never forgets His people that He was given. He prays for them there and He always watches over them.

Jesus is not here; he has risen, just as he said.
Matthew 28:6

Am I a gift for Jesus?

Are you a gift for Jesus? Don't you want to belong to someone as kind and loving as He is?

Jesus has said that if you come to Him, He will take even you to be His very own! This is called *salvation*. Ask Jesus to be your Saviour today!

**Jesus said, 'Let the little children come to me,
and do not hinder them.'
Matthew 19:14**

Salvation

Did you ever want to be *perfect?* What would that be like? You would be kind and good and helpful to everyone. You would never lie or say mean words. You would not even think bad thoughts!

**The Lord searches every heart
and understands every motive behind the thoughts.
1 Chronicles 28:9**

Imagine if you were always obedient (wouldn't your mum and dad be happy about that!)

You would always do what God's Bible told you to do and you would never do anything it told you not to do.

In other words, you would never *sin.*

Blessed ... are those who hear the word of God and obey it.
Luke 11:28

But most of the time you really don't want to be perfect, do you?

When your big brother (or sister or mum or dad) makes you angry, you want to say mean words, or hit. And it's hard to obey, isn't it?

You know you can't be perfect, not even for one day!

**If we claim to be without sin, we deceive ourselves
and the truth is not in us.
1 John 1:8**

Did you know that God is perfect and fair and has to punish every bad thing that is done? Did you know that God's **heaven** is a perfect and clean place, and only perfect people can go there? No sin is allowed.

Does this mean that you can never go to heaven? No! It doesn't!

The Lord Jesus loves His people very much and He wants them to come to heaven to be with Him. That is why He came to earth. He lived a perfect life for them and then died for them. He was punished for their sins so that they wouldn't have to be.

Jesus is the way to heaven!

**Jesus answered, 'I am the way and the truth and the life.
No-one comes to the Father except through me.'
John 14:6**

So how can *you* get to heaven? This is the most important question anyone will ever ask you. Do you know the answer? Jesus Himself must change you.

If you're all dirty and smelly, you can't come in to eat dinner without getting cleaned up and changing clothes.

Jesus must wash away all your filthy sin, so that you can come into God's holy heaven.

He makes you clean, inside and out.

Wash away all my iniquity and cleanse me from my sin.
Psalm 51:2

First, Jesus changes you on the inside. He sends the Holy Spirit to give you a new spiritual heart that wants to be saved. **Regeneration** is the big word for this.

But how do you know if you have a new heart? Well, if you do, there are certain things that will happen.

The first thing your new heart will do is **believe** what the Bible says about Jesus. Jesus did everything that had to be done for you to be saved.

He offers salvation as a **gift**!

Believe in the Lord Jesus, and you will be saved.
Acts 16:31

Did you pay your grandmother for the dolly or the truck that she gave you for your birthday?

No, silly! Then it wouldn't be a gift.

You don't have to buy salvation by giving God money or even by being extra good. Your believing heart will take the gift of Jesus and what He did.

This is also called having *faith*.

This righteousness from God comes through faith in Jesus Christ.
Romans 3:22

What is faith? Faith is knowing that only Jesus can save you. Faith is telling Him that you want this gift and that you want to be clean inside and outside.

But more than this, faith is your heart running to Jesus because there you will be safe. Your sin would keep you from God forever, but Jesus died for your sins and will forgive them.

God's little lambs run to the Good Shepherd, the Lord Jesus; they rest in His strong arms and He carries them safely to heaven.

You are all children of God through faith in Christ Jesus.
Galatians 3:26

Do you want Jesus to be your Saviour?

If you do, then you will be sorry for your **sins**, the bad things you do. This is called **repentance**. Jesus hates sins. He had to die so that God would forgive our sins.

Little children who love and trust Him are sad when they do wrong things. They hate sin and try hard to be good, because that pleases their Saviour.

Repent ... and turn to God, so that your sins may be wiped out.
Acts 3:19

Faith and *repentance* are two signs of a new heart and a clean inside.

Jesus also changes you on the outside. He takes off your dirty smelly sin and dresses you in His own obedience to God.

When God looks at you, He forgives you. He sees the nice clean obedience that Jesus has covered you with. This is called *justification.*

Since we have been justified through faith, we have peace with God through our Lord Jesus Christ. Romans 5:1

What is the family of God?

Do you know anyone who is **adopted?** When Jesus saves you, He makes you one of God's children. He takes you into the family of God.

Isn't it exciting to have God to be your **heavenly Father?**

This is the best family ever!

**'I will be a Father to you, and you will be my sons and daughters,'
says the Lord Almighty.
2 Corinthians 6:18**

All these changes and great things that God does for His children are called *salvation.* Isn't salvation wonderful? And there are even more blessings that God gives to you, if you are saved.

Jesus helps you more and more to turn from sin and to be good and obedient and to please Him. This is called *sanctification.* It lasts all your life.

And finally, when you get to heaven, all the changes will be finished. You will be perfect then! (The Bible calls this last change *glorification.*)

And you will sing songs to Jesus to thank Him for saving you.

Thanks be to God for his indescribable gift!
2 Corinthians 9:15

Has Jesus saved you?

If you're not sure, or you don't understand about salvation yet, it is very important for you to find out more.

Be sure to go to a church where you will hear God's preacher explain His word.

Ask all the questions you need to. Read God's Bible or have someone read it to you.

Jesus loves little children. Ask Jesus to change your heart today!

Everyone who calls on the name of the Lord will be saved.
Romans 10:13

MEMORY VERSES:

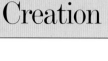

Creation

Get someone to test you to see how many verses you can remember! Tick a box when you have learnt a verse.

The heavens declare the glory of God; the skies proclaim the work of His hands. Psalm 19:1

We know that the whole creation has been groaning ... right up to the present time. Romans 8:22

In the beginning you laid the foundations of the earth. Psalm 102:25

God saw all that He had made, and it was very good. Genesis 1:31

By the word of the Lord were the heavens made. Psalm 33:6

With my great power... I made the earth and its people and the animals that are on it. Jeremiah 27:5

Know that the Lord is God. It is He who made us, and we are His. Psalm 100:3

So God created man in His own image... male and female He created them. Genesis 1:27

MEMORY VERSES:

Obey me, and I will be your God and you will be my people.
Jeremiah 7:23

Lead us not into temptation, but deliver us from the evil
one. Matthew 6:13

Sin entered the world through one man, and death through
sin. Romans 5:12

You know my folly, O God; my guilt is not hidden from you.
Psalm 69:5

You may be sure that your sin will find you out.
Numbers 32:23

For all have sinned and fall short of the glory of God.
Romans 3:23

Christ Jesus came into the world to save sinners.
1 Timothy 1:15

God demonstrates His own love for us in this:
While we were still sinners, Christ died for us. Romans 5:8

MEMORY VERSES:

The Father has sent His Son to be the Saviour of the world.
1 John 4:14

For the Father loves the Son and shows Him all He does.
John 5:20

They were yours; you gave them to me.
John 17:6

Father, I want those you have given me to be with me where I am, and to see my glory. John 17:24

Today in the town of David a Saviour has been born to you; He is Christ the Lord. Luke 2:11

They crucified him, along with the criminals.
Luke 23:33

Christ died for our sins.
1 Corinthians 15:3

Jesus is not here; He has risen, just as He said.
Matthew 28:6

Jesus said, 'Let the little children come to me, and do not hinder them.' Matthew 19:14

MEMORY VERSES:

The Lord searches every heart and understands every
motive behind the thoughts. 1 Chronicles 28:9

Blessed ... are those who hear the word of God and obey it.
Luke 11:28

If we claim to be without sin, we deceive ourselves and the
truth is not in us. 1 John 1:8

Jesus answered, 'I am the way and the truth and the life.
No-one comes to the Father except through me.' John 14:6

Wash away all my iniquity and cleanse me from my sin.
Psalm 51:2

Believe in the Lord Jesus, and you will be saved.
Acts 16:31

This righteousness from God comes through faith in
Jesus Christ. Romans 3:22

You are all children of God through faith in Christ Jesus.
Galatians 3:26

MEMORY VERSES:

Repent ... and turn to God, so that your sins may be wiped out. Acts 3:19

Since we have been justified through faith, we have peace with God through our Lord Jesus Christ. Romans 5:1

'I will be a Father to you, and you will be my sons and daughters,' says the Lord Almighty. 2 Corinthians 6:18

**Thanks be to God for his indescribable gift!
2 Corinthians 9:15**

**Everyone who calls on the name of the Lord will be saved.
Romans 10:13**

Look out for the other two books in this series

Beginning with God

God   The Bible   The Trinity

Living with God

Worship   Heaven

Obedience   Prayer